HOUSTON ROCKETS

AARON FRISCH

Published by Creative Education
P.O. Box 227
Mankato, Minnesota 56002
Creative Education is an imprint of The Creative Company.

DESIGN AND PRODUCTION BY ZENO DESIGN

PHOTOGRAPHS BY Getty Images (NBAE)

Copyright © 2008 Creative Education.
International copyright reserved in all countries.
No part of this book may be reproduced in any form
without written permission from the publisher.
Printed in the United States of America

LIBRARY OF CONGRESS CATALOGING-IN-PUBLICATION DATA

Frisch, Aaron.
Houston Rockets / by Aaron Frisch.
p. cm. — (NBA champions)
Includes index.
ISBN-13: 978-1-58341-507-8
1. Houston Rockets (Basketball team)—History.
2. Basketball—History. I. Title.

GV885.52.H68F755 2007
796.323'64097641411—dc22   2006020239

First edition

9 8 7 6 5 4 3 2 1

COVER PHOTO: *Guard Tracy McGrady*

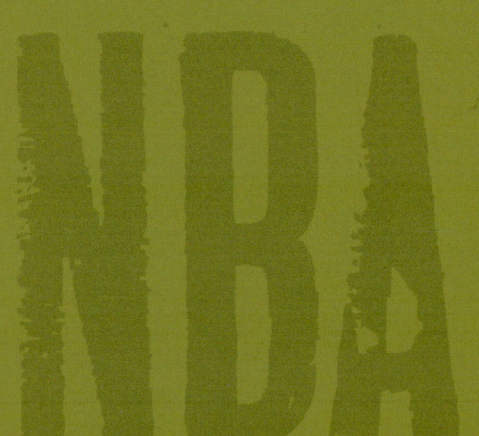

THE ROCKETS are a professional basketball team in the National Basketball Association (NBA). They play in Houston, Texas. Houston is one of the biggest cities in the United States.

Houston has lots of tall buildings called skyscrapers ▷

THE ROCKETS' arena is called the Toyota Center. Their uniforms are red, white, and silver. The Rockets play lots of games against teams called the Grizzlies, Hornets, Mavericks, and Spurs.

◀ The Rockets and Mavericks are both from Texas

THE ROCKETS played their first season in 1967. They started out in San Diego, California. They played four seasons in San Diego. Then they moved to Houston.

The Rockets were not a good team at first ▷

FORWARD Elvin Hayes was the Rockets' first star player. He was nicknamed "The Big E." Hayes was a tough rebounder and had a great jump shot. He played seven seasons for the Rockets.

◁ Elvin Hayes tried hard to get every rebound

CENTER Moses Malone was another famous Rockets player. He was good at rebounding and won an award as the NBA's best player in 1979. But Houston still could not win the NBA championship.

Moses Malone played in the NBA for 19 years ▷

IN THE 1980S, the Rockets added centers Ralph Sampson and Hakeem Olajuwon (oh-LAH-joo-won). They were both more than seven feet (213 cm) tall. Fans called them the "Twin Towers." Olajuwon and Sampson played their best, but Houston still lost in the playoffs.

◁ It was very hard to score against the Twin Towers

IN 1994, the Rockets finally won their first NBA championship. Sampson was gone, but Olajuwon was better than ever. In 1995, the Rockets beat a team called the Magic four games in a row to win the championship again!

Hakeem Olajuwon led Houston to the NBA championship ▷

AFTER Olajuwon left Houston, the Rockets got another center. His name was Yao *(YAH-oh)* Ming. He was almost seven and a half feet (232 cm) tall! Ming was the greatest basketball player ever to come from China.

◁ Yao Ming was good at shooting one-handed shots

TRACY McGRADY was another good Rockets player. He was a guard who could jump high and score in lots of ways. The Rockets have many new players today. Houston fans hope that their team will win the NBA championship again soon!

Fans called Tracy McGrady "T-Mac" for short ▷

GLOSSARY

ARENA   a building with lots of seats where teams play basketball

NATIONAL BASKETBALL ASSOCIATION (NBA)
a group of basketball teams that play against each other; there are 30 teams in the NBA today

PLAYOFFS   games that are played after the season to see which team is the best

PROFESSIONAL   a person or team that gets paid to play or work

FUN FACTS

TEAM COLORS: Red, white, and silver

HOME ARENA: Toyota Center

CONFERENCE/DIVISION: Western Conference, Southwest Division

FIRST SEASON: 1967

NBA CHAMPIONSHIPS: 1994, 1995

GREAT PLAYERS: Elvin Hayes (forward), Hakeem Olajuwon (center), Tracy McGrady (guard)

NBA WEB SITE FOR KIDS: http://www.nba.com/kids/

TEAM NAME: The Rockets got their name because space rockets used to be built in San Diego. San Diego is where the team played its first seasons.

INDEX

Hayes, Elvin 11, 23
Malone, Moses 12
McGrady, Tracy 21, 23
Ming, Yao 19
NBA championships 16, 23
Olajuwon, Hakeem 15, 16, 19, 23
playoffs 15
Sampson, Ralph 15, 16
San Diego, California 8, 23
team colors 7, 23
Toyota Center 7, 23
"Twin Towers" 15